Quick & Smart Entrepreneur's Handbook
From the Procedures to Prevent Problems Series

by

Adrienne Heard

Hollandays Publishing Corp.
Dayton, Ohio
www.hollandays.net

◆ ◆ ◆

To order additional copies, contact the publisher:

Hollandays Publishing Corp.
714 East Monument Avenue
Dayton, Ohio 45402
937.898.2520 or www.hollandays.net

International Standard Book Number
(ISBN) 0-9708224-6-4

Printed in the United States of America
1ˢᵗ Printing

◆ ◆ ◆

Management problems are the number one reason for business failures. This book is a collection of successful management clues to help you succeed.

One of the greatest developmental challenges you face as an entrepreneur is that you don't know what you don't know. With that in mind I encourage you to read this book from cover to cover. Once you know what you don't know, you can use the resource section as a guide to additional training and development in those specific areas.

Success to you – on your terms.

Adrienne Heard
President, Heard Management

With special thanks to the members of eWomenNetwork, Dayton, Ohio Chapter

◆ ◆ ◆

Foreword
Using this book

This volume is meant to be used, and used often:

- **The management clues** that make up the main text may introduce you to business ideas or simply remind you of important steps to take as you run your business every day.
- **The resources** guide you to the best websites and books for entrepreneurs.
- **The Take Action activities** get you prepared. Try an activity or two from each challenge and find out now – is owning a business or managing a business for others a good step?
- **The note pages** are your space. Whether you attend one of Ms. Heard's seminars and use the pages to jot down key points, or you read the book and use the pages for reminders, plans, and the occasional dream ~ use the note pages to make the book your own.

One of the most important ideas in business is to keep it simple. We think this handbook does just that. So use it, enjoy it, and prosper.

- Editor

◆ ◆ ◆

Contents

Challenges

◆ ◆ ◆

1
Challenge

First Things First

Focus

Your mission statement
and core competencies
will help define your focus.

If it's important to you to be a leader in the volunteer community, this might not be the time to start a business.

Community involvement is a form of networking...but it also takes a lot of time.

Goal?
Write it down!

The first step in setting goals is writing them.

After you write them DON'T file them. Allow those goals to motivate you by keeping them posted at your desk. Their visibility will be a constant reminder of what you need to do.

Do what you know.

The best business opportunity is when you can get paid for doing something you enjoy so much that you'd be willing to do it for free.

Write Your Airplane Definition

How would you describe your business to an interested person sitting next to you on an airplane?

Write a short, to the point explanation that includes product, market, business mission. . . and what makes you different than your competition.

Airplane Definition Example:

Heard Management (HM) offers business management consulting services to small businesses that are ready to change. Using training and experience from a variety of workplace settings, HM develops management tools to help entrepreneurs succeed. The emphasis is on "Procedures to Prevent Problems".

Gut feelings

and

intuition

are often just your subconscious thoughts comparing notes.

Do some research to prove what your subconscious is trying to tell you.

If it seems too good to be true . .
It's probably too good to be true.

Read the fine print.

Be clear about your core competency.

What is your unique selling point?

How are you different
than your competitors?

(Price can't be the only difference)

Example:

Core Competencies for Heard Management

1. *Communicates complex concepts in non-complex terms.*

2. *Provides education and support in a variety of business arenas.*

Have a mission statement.
Why does your business exist?

(Don't get this confused
with your personal mission statement.)

Example:

Mission Statement for Heard Management

The mission of Heard Management is to increase the probability of success for small businesses by enhancing the management knowledge and skills of entrepreneurs as well as increasing their access to appropriate resources.

Plan to get rich.
But plan to have fun, too.

❖ ❖ ❖

Have a dream.
Believe in your dream.
Think about how to achieve your dream.
Do it!

Challenge 1 References
First Things First

Books:
- *Small Time Operator* by Bernard Kamoroff
- *The Small Business Resource Guide* by Gene Fairbrother
- *How to Start, Finance, and Manage Your Own Small Business* by Joseph R. Mancuso

Websites:
- SBA.gov
- Americanexpress.com
- Inc.com

Take Action:
- Interview an entrepreneur (not a competitor).
- Attend a Small Business Administration (SBA) prebusiness seminar.
- Make a list of everyone you know who might help you – as a customer, employee, banker, or supporter.
- Discuss your idea with some kind but honest friends. Their feedback will be valuable.
- Develop your airplane definition.

Challenge

2

Planning Basics

If you fail to plan,
you plan to fail.

A **business plan is the foundation** for your

- Operating guide
- Strategic marketing plan
- Personnel and financial plans
- Company's working model

Know your strengths and weaknesses.

Manage your weaknesses.

Excel using your strengths.

A **business plan is the foundation** for your operating guide.

Entrepreneurs must set realistic goals and determine how to use the resources of the business to achieve those goals.

The 4 P's of Marketing
P_{roduct}
P_{lace}
P_{rice}
$P_{romotion}$

Miss just one and your product stays on the shelf.

A business plan is the foundation
for a **strategic marketing plan**.

A business plan
is built on market research.

Without customers,
you don't have a business plan.

FLAW Insurance

*Every business
should have 4 kinds of insurance:*

Fire

Liability

Automobile

Worker's compensation

**A business plan
is the foundation
for personnel and financial plans:**

❖   You need both.

❖   You have to plan to meet
     your personnel needs.

❖   You have to establish budgets
     based on your business
     situation.

Learn from the mistakes of others.
It's less expensive than
making all the mistakes yourself.

A business plan
is a working model of your business.

**A good business plan allows you to play
"what if?" on paper.**
(It's cheaper that way.)

Measure Twice. Cut Once.

❖ ❖ ❖

Assuming is the mother of all mistakes.

A business plan
can be a financing proposal:

A financing proposal based
on a business plan is a powerful tool.

It will demonstrate
that there is a need for funds,
that the funds will
further the success of the business,
and
that there is an obvious
source of repayment of the funds.

Your **operating plan**
contains the written procedures and guidelines for implementing your business plan.

Writing a plan to show others?
**Give enough information
to understand your plan,**
not enough to operate your plan.

*A business plan
should be no more than 15 pages.*

*Anything more is
research, supporting detail or fluff.*

The **3** parts to a business plan are:

- **Words** (Business Description)
- **Numbers** (Financials)
- **Proof** (Supporting Documents)

All three parts must agree.

Changes will always happen.
Your goal is to be prepared, not perfect.

❖   ❖   ❖

Don't make a wish.
Make a plan!

Do it Right Steps

1. Determine how to do it right.

2. Document how to do it right.

3. Distribute the news about how to do it right.

4. Reward those who do it right.

5. Take action on those who won't do it right.

Think it will take 2 hours?
Plan on 6.
It's always going to take longer
than you thought.
Take your estimate and multiply by three.

❖ ❖ ❖

A crisis will always occur ~
have good contingency plans.

Risk Management

1. Define the problem

2. Determine the consequences

3. Evaluate the alternatives

4. Choose an alternative

5. Act

6. Evaluate

Strategic Planning:
Always work from a list.
Write it out, organize it,
and work on your most important task.

❖ ❖ ❖

People don't plan to fail.
They just fail to plan.

Challenge 2 References
Planning Basics

Books:
- The Business Planning Guide by David H. Bangs

Websites:
- SBA.gov
- Inc.com
- Score.org

Take Action:
- Outline a business plan.
- Establish a timeline for your plan.
- Investigate the advantages and disadvantages of sole proprietorship, partnership and incorporation.
- Describe the perfect location for your business. Why would it be perfect?
- List everything you need (and don't need) in a location (must have/can do without).
- Research your location – do a traffic count, investigate taxes, list competitors, check out available utilities, investigate availability of labor, seek information on zoning, and evaluate the safety of the property and neighborhood.
- If you need a location, talk to a realtor about going rates and locations.
- Talk to an insurance agent. Get an estimate on the costs for the various policies you would need.
- Attend a meeting of a professional organization related to your business.
- Take a banker to lunch.

3

Challenge

Paperwork

W*hy keep records?*

❖ *Uncle Sam wants to see them.*
❖ *The bank won't loan without them.*
❖ *Good managers use them.*

What's the difference between data and information?

Data is a collection of facts.

Information is data that's been interpreted for use.

Unfortunately, most of us are constantly being bombarded by useless data that doesn't really give us any information.

*Write instructions
for common procedures and processes.*

*It saves everyone time,
particularly new employees.*

Have a management audit performed.

A management audit is similar to a financial audit – except your management procedures are reviewed instead of your accounting procedures.

Act
on an item
the first time you touch it.

Get organized now.

Does this document require action?
Complete, delegate, or
put in the tickler file
with an action date.

Is this document
for information only?
Pass it, file it, or toss it.

Write it down.
Would you rather argue
"I said..." vs. "You said..."
OR
"Here's what was written and signed."

Every keystroke is
another opportunity for error.
Use a common database
whenever possible.

Don't use computers
to do things that can be done
efficiently by hand.

Don't use hands
to do things that can be done
efficiently by a computer.

15 pages?
Don't fax it. Mail it.
Otherwise you'll tie up my machine,
Use up my paper,
And waste my time sorting.

❖ ❖ ❖

No job is over until the paperwork is done.

Challenge 3 References
Paperwork

Books
- *Small Time Operator* by Bernard Kamoroff
- *Small Business Legal Guide* by Robert Friedman
- *Starting A Business & Keeping Records,* IRS Publication 583

Websites:
- Toolkit.cch.com
- BusinessLaw.gov
- FTC.gov
- IRS.ustreas.gov

Take Action:
- Organize your home records.
- Order IRS Publication 583. (It's free!)
- Stroll through the recordkeeping section of your neighborhood business supply store. Check out forms, books, and software for recordkeeping.

Challenge 4

Money & Time

*Learn to listen
to your financial statements.*

Don't lie to the bank.

The need to be creative with your banker
is the first clue
that you're lying to yourself
about your business.

Personal Debt

Spending money you don't have
to buy things you don't need
to impress people you don't like.

Business Debt
Spending money you don't have
to buy things you need
to generate more money.

Equity purchases part of a business.
Its cost is loss of control
and a share of the profits.

❖ ❖ ❖

Debt is a loan to be repaid.
Its cost? Interest.

Interest is the cost of money.
(the bank's money = debt)
◆ Purchase the right product (line of credit, short term loan or long term loan)
◆ Purchase at the best cost (lowest interest rate)

❖ ❖ ❖

5 C's of Credit

Don't know what they are**?**

Your banker does.

5 C's of Credit

Character

Collateral

Conditions

Capital

Capacity

The bank
is interested in your **CHARACTER.**

- Do you keep your word?
- Have you ever promised to pay someone – and broken that promise (paid late or filed bankruptcy)?
- Do you obey the law?
- Have you ever been arrested or convicted of a crime?
- Are you honest with your government obligations?
- Have you filed income taxes and other appropriate documents?

Your banker will want to know
about your
COLLATERAL.

Banks aren't in the business of selling houses and
used equipment.

Collateral is just a security blanket (or last resort)
for the bank to try to recover a portion of the funds
they loaned you - if the worst happens.

You and your banker need to know
the **CONDITIONS** of the economy
and your industry.

If either is down, the risk
of investing in your business is greater.

Your banker will want to know about your **CAPITAL.**

How much are you putting in the business? You and your investors must assume part of the risk. If you're not willing to invest in the business, why should the bank take a chance?

What is the net worth of your business?

Your banker is interested
in your **CAPACITY.**

How much of your profit
is already being used to pay off loans?

How much of your profit
can be used to pay off new debt?

Have six months
of working capital in reserve
(or in a line of credit)
when you start.

❖ ❖ ❖

Keep your business funds
separate from your personal funds.
Write checks to transfer money
between accounts.

CASH FLOW
Be Prepared!
You'll have to pay your staff,
your suppliers and your overhead
(rent, phones, etc.)
long before you'll receive payment
for services performed.

❖ ❖ ❖

Failure to plan for cash flow
can close a profitable business.

10 Ways to Improve Cash Flow

1. Develop a short-term (3 months) and long-term (12 months) plan.
2. Add late charges and fees when possible.
3. Pay bills on the due date unless there is a discount for early payment.
4. Reduce your inventory to include only necessary items.
5. Sell slow moving items at cost.
6. Lease instead of purchase equipment.
7. Make bank deposits promptly.
8. Purchase equipment, supplies and inventory prudently.
9. Increase sales.
10. Increase prices.

Rent is due on the first of the month.

How much cash do you receive in sales on the first day of each month

?

To Buy or Not to Buy . . .
When you are thinking of adding tools, equipment and/or employees, look at each item in light of these three key points:

1. Will it increase sales?

2. Will it decrease your overhead percentage?

3. Will it give you time to do other things?

If you cannot answer YES to all three,
rethink the need.

Use this test to identify the real
needs and eliminate just the wants.

%
tells more than
$
when you're managing your business.

A penny saved is a penny earned.
Increase your bottom line
by spending wisely.

❖ ❖ ❖

Cheap is expensive.

If you don't have time
to do it right . . .
When are you going to find time
to do it over?

How much is your time worth?

It might be time-wise and dollar-wise to pay someone else to do it. Then you can use your time for strategic planning, marketing, managing or building energy reserves.

❖ ❖ ❖

Lean Thinking:
If it's not necessary, don't do it.

Challenge 4 Resources
Money & Time

Books:
- *Small Time Operator* by Bernard Kamoroff
- *Small Business Legal Guide* by Robert Friedman
- *Starting A Business & Keeping Records*, IRS Publication 583
- *The Basics of Budgeting* by Terry Dickey

Websites:
- SBA.gov
- Viacorp.com/DebtBook.html
- Tannedfeet.com
- Isquare.com
- Inc.com

Take Action
- Make a list of what you need to get your business started. Price each item.
- Track your personal expenses. How much do you need to live on? How will you pay your personal expenses while your business is getting off the ground?
- Develop a budget for your business.
- Attend a one day workshop on understanding financial statements.

5

Challenge

Who's Buying?

*Word of mouth
only works after you've gotten
your first satisfied customer.
Have a marketing plan to get that first customer.*

❖ ❖ ❖

Satisfied people don't change.

Listen to what your customers are saying.

❖ ❖ ❖

Know your arena of performance.
Business
Personal
Politics
Academia
Government
Military
Entertainment
Church
Community Service/Non-Profit
Different arenas have different rules.
Be sure you follow the rules
of your arena.

What are you selling?

This is not the same as
"What are your products or services?"
People buy
solutions *to their problems*
and
satisfaction
of their needs.

Know your product.
When you go in to see the purchasing agent,
don't ask,
"What does your organization buy?"

Be prepared to tell the agent
what your company sells
(product or service) and ask,
*"Which of your departments could possibly
use this product/service?"*

"With whom should I speak?"

A contract does not equal money.
Read the wording carefully.
A contract could be for purchase of goods/services
as needed.
If the need doesn't come up,
then no purchases will be made.

Don't offer credit – accept VISA or MasterCard.

The fees you'll pay to accept a bankcard are much less than the headaches you'll encounter trying to monitor and collect on house credit.

Make sure your market will last at least as long as your bank loan.

❖ ❖ ❖

Describe your perfect customer. Then go out and find him or her.

There's no such thing as no competition.
If you think you have no competition,
you don't really know your market.

❖ ❖ ❖

The internet and mail order catalogues
might be your competition.

Make new friends, but keep the old.
One is silver and the other gold.

❖   ❖   ❖

A good customer
is your company's best friend.

A Good Customer

- Understands your product line
- Knows your company
- Buys regularly
- Buys a variety of your products
- Buys a large quantity of your products
- Pays promptly
- Is pleased
- Tells others

Goal: Keep this customer.

What does your customer want?
A quality product
At a competitive price
At the right time & place

An "OK" Customer:

Knows a product
Knows your company
Buys occasionally
Buys one product
Pays slowly
Is satisfied
Goal: Develop into a Good Customer.

It's easier to develop a current customer than to find a new customer.

❖   ❖   ❖

A Borderline Customer:
- Thinks he or she knows the product (but doesn't)
- Seldom buys anything
- Pays eventually – after much effort
- Is seldom satisfied
- Complains to others

Goal: Evaluate if an effort should be made to shift to okay status or ex-customer status.

Challenge 5 Resources
Who's Buying

Books:
- *The Market Planning Guide* by David H. Bangs, Jr.

Websites:
- Knowthis.com
- Selltoairforce.org
- FTC.gov
- Marketingsource.com

Take Action:
- Shop the competition, in person and on the internet.
- Describe your perfect customer.
- Write out where and how you will find the perfect customer.
- Write out where and how your perfect customer will find you.

6

Challenge

People

Network.
Time is precious, so use it wisely.

❖ ❖ ❖

Exchanging business cards?
Note the date and place you met
on the face of the card . . . and anything else
that will help you remember the person.

When in doubt . . . ask!

❖ ❖ ❖

*When explaining anything,
first describe
the problem it is designed to solve.*

Return all phone calls
within 2 working days.

Leaving a voice mail message?

· Always give your phone number - your customer might be away from the office when she receives the message.

· Say your phone number slowly - she needs time to write it down.

Making a phone call?
Plan what you want to say
before you make the phone call.

Smile when you're on the phone.
Yes, the person on the other end
can hear your smile.

They can also hear typing on the
keyboard,
flipping through a magazine,
and snacking.

Publicity is free advertising . . .
but, only if it's positive.

Telephone Dating

Make a telephone appointment when you want to have a focused conversation with someone who is often busy. Confirm the date, time, length of appointment, and location (i.e. home office).

Power:
Knowing how to inspire greatness in others.

Employees are your greatest investment.

◆ Value and maintain employees just as you would an expensive piece of equipment.

◆ Invest wisely. Hire the right person for the right job.

◆ Use properly. Follow job procedures, descriptions and employee handbook.

◆ Maintain properly. Maintain good working conditions and equipment.

◆ Upgrade to remain current in the industry. Provide ongoing training.

Employees should read your handbook and sign a statement that they have read and understood the rules.

Hire based on JOB requirements
. . . not because you have a friend
or family member
who needs a job.

*Opinions are worth what you pay for them.
Don't ask a friend.
PAY a professional.*

All lawyers are not created equal.

You wouldn't expect an eye doctor
to do foot surgery, would you?
Use a business attorney.

The three P's of business
Production
Promotion
Paperwork
Make sure someone is accountable
for each P.

3 P's

Production
Promotion
Paperwork

If you're not good at all three, be prepared to pay someone else.

If you're too busy to do all three, be prepared to pay someone else.

If you don't like doing all three, be prepared to pay someone else.

Solve problems while they're small.

❖ ❖ ❖

*It isn't the people you fire
who make your life miserable . . .
it's the people you don't.*

Management

- Who does what
- Who reports to whom
- Where the buck stops
- Who makes the final decision

Surround yourself with GIANTS and learn from them!

Challenge 6 Resources
People

Books:
- *Small Time Operator* by Bernard Kamoroff
- *How to Start, Finance, and Manage Your Own Small Business* by Joseph R. Mancuso
- *Human Resources* by Jill A. Rossiter
- *Occupational Outlook Handbook* by U.S. Department of Labor

Websites:
- SBA.gov
- Toolkit.cch.com
- All-biz.com
- Inc.com
- Salary.com
- OSHA.gov

Take Action:
- Develop a standard voice mail message for your business.
- Write a job description.
- Describe the perfect employee for each job at your business.
- Write out where and how you will find the perfect employee. How much will that employee cost?
- Write out the reasons that the perfect employee would accept this position.

7 Challenge

Final Thoughts

*Have a passion for what you do!
Sometimes to stay in business
you might have to work for free
after you've paid your other bills.*

Increase your daily success!

· Start your day with a plan of action.

· Stay in balance with your life.

· Be neat.

· Get real rest.

· Take a lunch break.

If you don't have written documentation
to prove your business exists,
then you don't have a business.
You have a hobby.

Interest:
Doing something
when it's convenient for you.

Commitment:
doing something
even when it's inconvenient.

Whatever is necessary
whenever it's convenient.
vs.
Whatever is necessary
whenever it's needed.

Airplane Definition
Print your brief business description
on a card to keep in your wallet.
Post a copy on the sun visor of your car too!

The 5 Knows of Business

1. Know your customer.
2. Know your competition.
3. Know your product.
4. Know your staffing requirements.
5. Know yourself.

Uncomfortable situations are opportunities for growth.

*If you want the rainbow,
you have to put up with the rain.*

*Every business
is a work in progress.*

There's no such thing as,
"I can't."

That just means either,
"I don't know how,"
or
"I won't."

Both can be remedied.

Nothing can guarantee success.

Stuff happens.
Have a contingency plan.

FOCUS

Select ONE business idea
at a time to develop.

Select ONE target market
at a time to develop.

Select ONE customer at a time to develop.

Select ONE product at a time to develop.

Do it well.

Then add your next product, customer,
target market, or business idea.

How fast you develop is your decision.

Do it now!

Challenge 7 Resources
Final Thoughts

Books:
- *Small Time Operator* by Robert Kamoroff
- *The Small Business Resource Guide* by Gene Fairbrother

Websites:
- SBA.gov
- All-biz.com
- Americanexpress.com
- Tannedfeet.com
- Inc.com
- Score.org

Take Action:
- Determine your core competency.
- Attend a business plan development workshop.
- Write a business plan (use your outline from Challenge 2).
- Memorize your airplane definition.

Resources

Websites ~ www.

- **All-biz.com**
  Business information sorted by industry and topic

- **Americanexpress.com**
  General information on entrepreneur challenges

- **Businessfinance.com**
  Information on where and how to find capital

- **BusinessLaw.gov**
  Legal and regulatory information
  Federal, state and local laws that affect day-to-day operations

- **FTC.gov**
  US Federal Trade Commission
  "How-to" site for consumer oriented businesses

- **Inc.com**
  Getting started and growing your business
  Human resources
  Finance & capital
  Sales

- **IRS.ustreas.gov**
  IRS tax information for business

- **Isquare.com**
  Tax tips for small businesses

Websites, con't.

- **Knowthis.com**
  Marketing basics, research, plans
  International marketing
  Advertising & promotion
  Marketing virtual library

- **Marketingsource.com**
  Marketing tools - both traditional and internet

- **OSHA.gov**
  Occupational Safety and Health Administration

- **Salary.com**
  Job summaries
  Pay ranges by geographic area

- **Sba.gov**
  (US Small Business Administration home page)
  Starting your business
  Business plans
  Financing your business
  Local and national resources

- **Score.org**
  Service Corps of Retired Executives
  On-line counseling from people who know business at no
  charge (funded through SBA)

Websites, con't.

- **Selltoairforce.org**
  Procedures for selling to the Air Force

- **Tannedfeet.com**
  Entrepreneur's Help Page: Business law, finance and business management

- **Toolkit.cch.com**
  Start-up tools
  Business tools
  Human Resources tools
  Reference books
  Legal information
  Tax information

- **Viacorp.com/DebtBook.html**
  How to collect business debts

Books

Bangs, David H., Jr. *The Business Planning Guide.* Upstart Publishing Company. Chicago, 1998.

Bangs, David H., Jr. *The Market Planning Guide.* Upstart Publishing Company. Chicago, 1998.

Dickey, Terry. *The Basics of Budgeting.* Crisp Publications, Inc. Menlo Park, California, 1992.

Fairbrother, Gene. *The Small Business Resource Guide.* National Association for the Self-Employed. Hurst, Texas, 1991.

Friedman, Robert. *Small Business Legal Guide.* Upstart Publishing Company. Chicago, 1998.

Kamoroff, Bernard. *Small Time Operator.* Bell Springs Publishing. Laytonville, California, 1993.

Mancuso, Joseph. *How to Start, Finance, and Manage Your Own Small Business.* Simon and Schuster. New York, 1984.

Rossiter, Jill. *Human Resources.* Upstart Publishing Company. Chicago, 1996.

United States Department of Labor. *Occupational Outlook Handbook.* Washington, D.C., updated annually.

United State Department of Treasury. *Publication 583: Starting a Business and Keeping Records.* Washington, D.C., updated annually.

ABOUT THE AUTHOR

Adrienne Heard is a management consultant offering services to businesses that are ready to change. Her services include individual coaching as well as lectures, seminars and classes.

Ms. Heard has an MBA in Management and Finance from the University of Dayton and a BA in Personnel Management/Business Administration from Michigan State University. Prior to forming Heard Management, Ms. Heard established a career in management with a number of Fortune 500 companies as well as with not-for-profit and privately-held firms. Heard Management was formed in 1993 to provide these same management and finance services on a consulting basis.

~ Notes ~

◆◆◆

~ *Notes* ~

♦♦♦

~ *Notes* ~

•••

~ *Notes* ~

~ *Notes* ~

◆◆◆

~ *Notes* ~

◆◆◆

~ *Notes* ~

◆◆◆

~ Notes ~

♦♦♦

~ Notes ~

•••

~ *Notes* ~

♦♦♦

To order additional copies of
Quick and Smart Entrepreneur's Handbook
or to contact Ms. Heard
about speaking at your business event

Call 1-800-792-3537 or write
bsmith@hollandays.net

Additional copies are $11.95 and prices do not
include shipping and handling. Discounted prices
for quantity orders are available.

◆ ◆ ◆

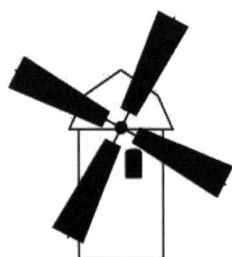